SEASIDE

what came with wave

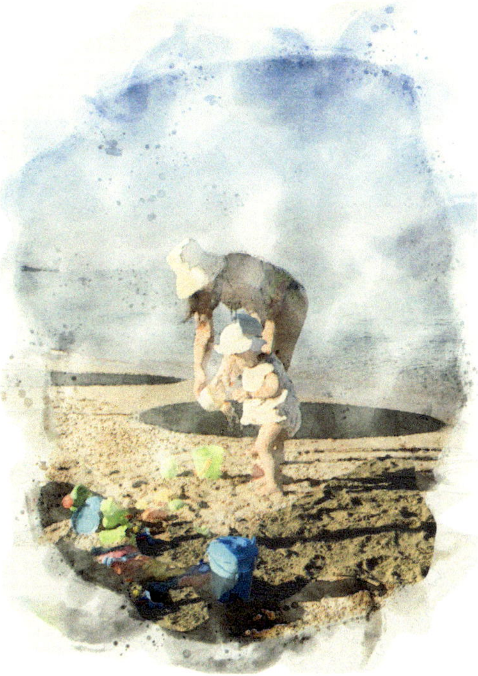

Dedication: To Mama

Seaside : what came with wave
Staples of British beach holidays, illustrated and told in verse.

Published by LANDE Jewels, 2024
ISBN 9781917579087
LANDE Jewels turns everyday pastimes into exciting and informative adventures.
www.landejewels.com

Moral rights asserted. A CIP catalogue record for this book is available from the British Library.

Contents

Inspired by beach holidays.

Prologue

The weather isn't guaranteed
In any part of England.
The forecast rarely predicts
How long the clouds will linger.

When packing up for a day trip
To nearby seaside town,
The mother took Wellington boots,
Rain covers, thermos flasks.

Equipped with tools—bucket and spade
And eager for adventure
We'd hunt for treasures in the shade
And think up shell-art ventures.

The chilly waters and seaweed
At times were a deterrent,
Save for unprecedented heat
When trippers were determined.

The mud, the shingle and the sand,
In daily 'hide and seek',
Would trick the voyagers' swim plans
When water would retreat.

When tide returned, we'd pack in haste
And head for fish and chips,
Fight off the squawking air-thieves
And eat soft serve ice cream.

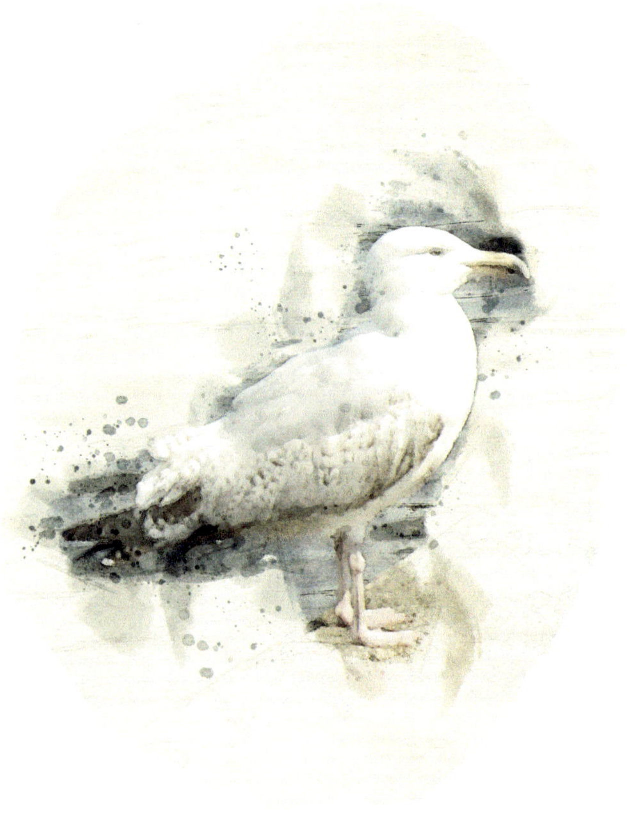

Inspired by seagull.

Air Thieves

What language wasn't heard on beaches
When seagull charged on fish and chips
Of unsuspecting, hungry creature
En route to savour their fill.

The birds roam blankets, rummage rucksacks,
Scare off the children from their lunch,
Intimidate with 'ha-ha-ha' sounds,
Chase one another for the scraps.

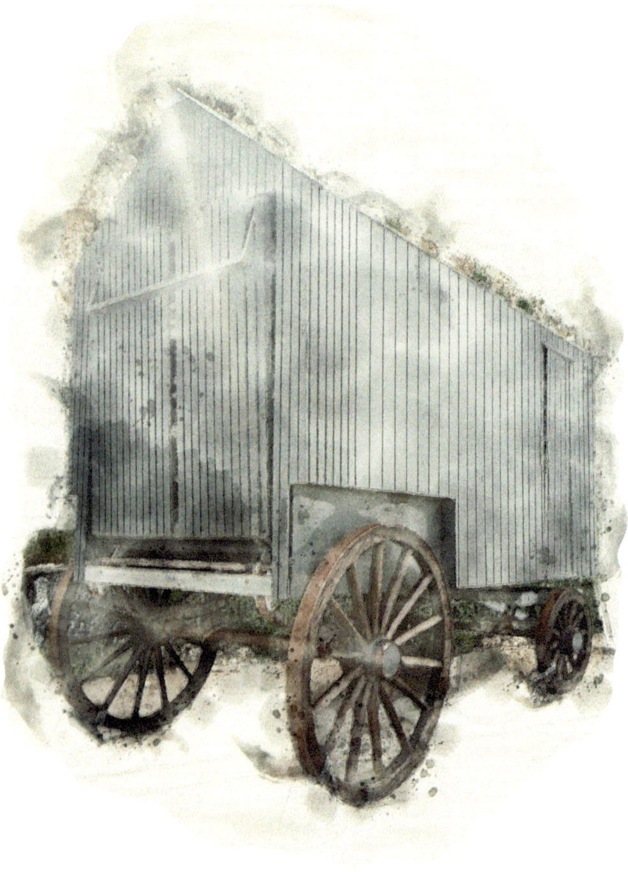

Inspired by bathing machine in Margate.

Bathing Machine

The prudish generations of Victorians
Came up with a response to a health craze—
To take the waters, with sufficient coverage,
The canvas hood or the machine to bathe.

The wooden sheds on wheels dotted the seaside,
Some were austere, the others were top notch,
Featuring dressing table, chair and drapery,
And stocked with perfumes, toiletries and robes.

Beach etiquette demanded segregation
Of men and women—60 feet apart.
The ladies were required to have swimwear—
A bulky, multilayered woolen garb.

The visitor would sign up for adventure,
Pay fee and wait, in patience, their turn.
Once called, they'll enter curious contraption,
Heading for water, pulled by men or horse.

Victorian swimmers hardly had the skillset,
The vast majority knew nothing of the sport,
Relying on the help of sturdy dippers,
Who'd pull them out of water in a shot.

1901 saw end of separation,
Bathing machines were few by WW1.
Bewildering today's holidaymakers,
They deck the beach of Osbourne and Margate.

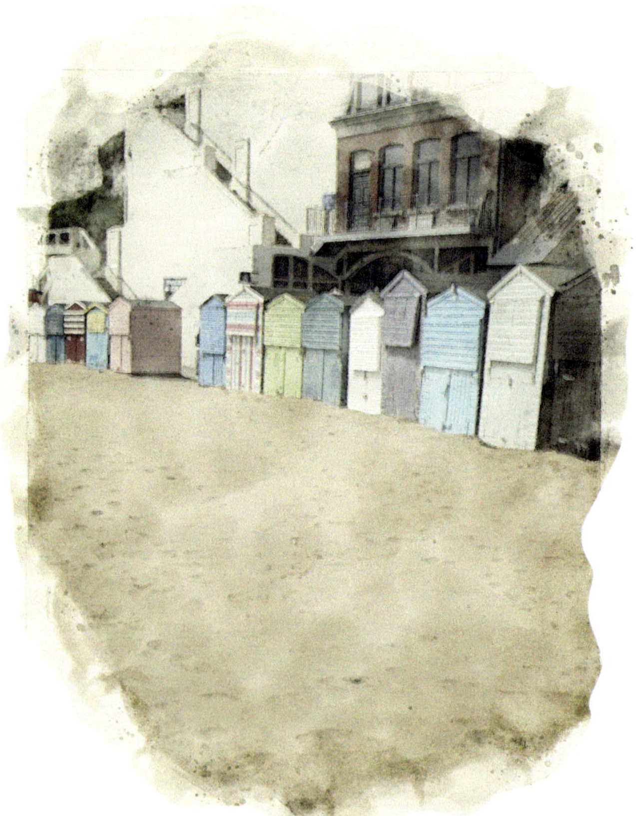

Inspired by beach huts in Broadstairs.

Beach Hut

An army of colourful huts
Fronts the meandering beachside,
With artwork and in vintage tints,
They brighten else wise chaste shoreline.

With Spartan space for couch and kitchen,
They open their doors up wide,
Revealing water sports equipment
Quietly waiting for right tide.

Majority of sheds on bricks
Have no basic facilities,
So if communal plumbing fails
North Sea acts as convenience.

With waiting lists, the rent or purchase
Of lumber cabins is a price.
The market hints at bubble cooking
For quintessential seaside.

With dire weather half the year,
They pass as no-heat rain refuge,
That is, if they withstand the gale winds,
The raging storms and tidal swings.

Popular with graffiti types
And young torch-bearing hooligans,
The heritage with upkeep high
Is kept dear by families.

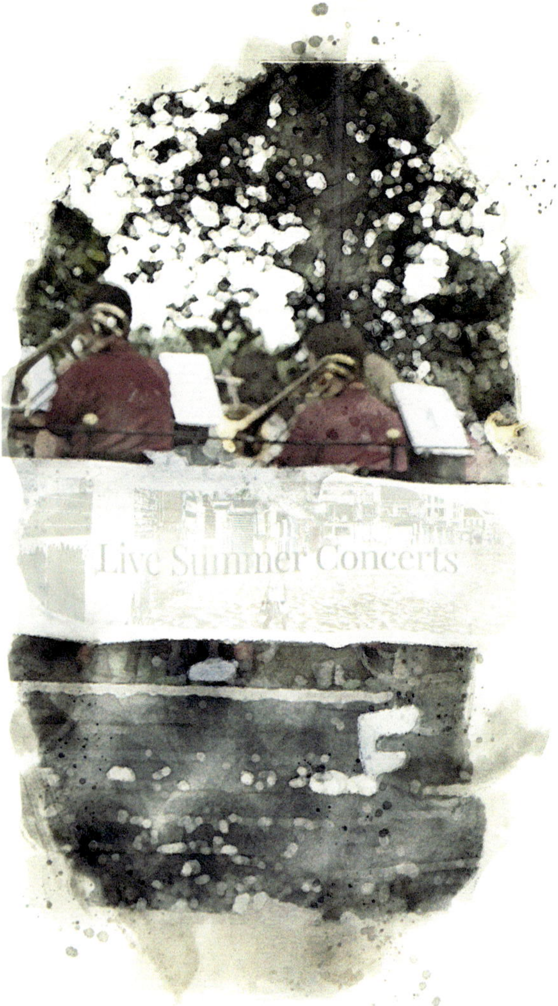

Inspired by live performance in Bandstand.

Brass Band in Bandstand

In order to promote the outdoor pastime
Attention was devoted to the parks,
The grounds for recreation, pleasure gardens—
All featuring ornately made bandstand.

Encouraging 'a better use of Sundays'
That 'will improve the urban dwellers' lives',
The virtue stalwarts of Victoriana
We're keen to secure local music acts.

Pavilions were built in their thousands,
They served as both a shelter and a stage,
Positioning the band as an attraction
And giving it a roof in case of rain.

Appealing to romantic, finer feelings,
The brass-band movement took UK by storm,
Proliferating up and down the country,
Bringing the gaiety of sounds to the seashore.

The tragic fate befell flamboyant structures—
The WW2 required railings' stock;
The ironwork was melted down for weapons
Or, as some say, dropped down instead of bombs.

The post war rise of TV screen and cinema
Cut short demand for bandstands' interplay.
Restored with conservationists' endeavours,
They welcome bands and their modern ways.

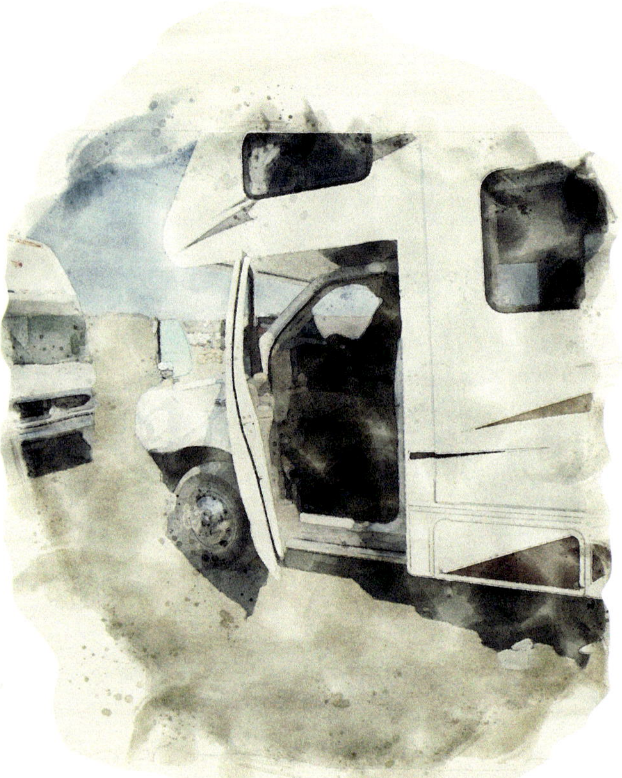

Inspired by a caravan.

Caravan

Taking its name from moving groups of travellers,
Along trade routes in deserts and Silk Road,
It featured in the Medieval merchant voyages
And helped to transport monarchs and convoys.

In 19th century, the horse-drawn single dwelling,
A 'Wanderer', complete in finest wood,
Was offered to the upper class exclusively
Who, by the travel prospects, had been wooed.

Post WW1, the deal became affordable,
However, the uptake was rather slow.
Industry boomed in aftermath of WW2
And since continued its persistent growth.

Whether a home or means to have more leisure,
The cars frequent the scenic camping parks
Or stay by shore equipped for any weather
In a seclusion of a quaint carpark.

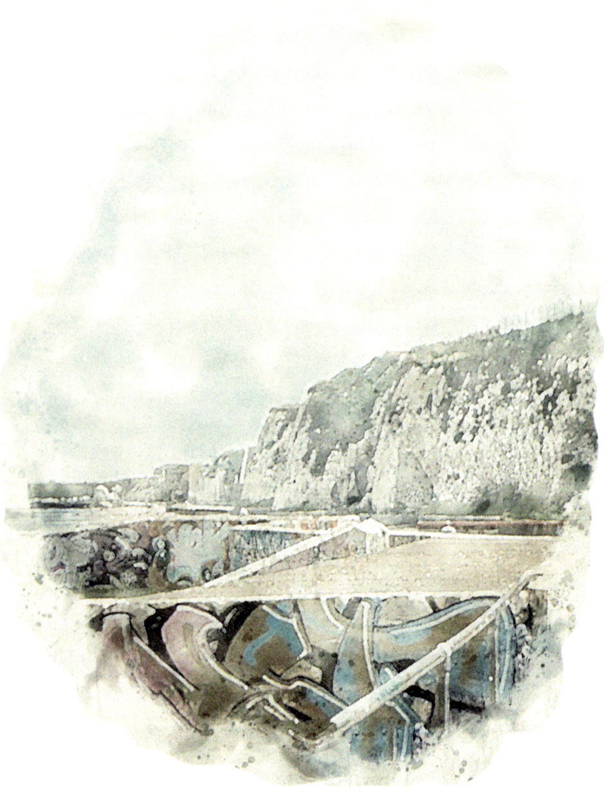

Inspired by a cliffs of Thanet coast.

Cliffs

Hundreds of thousands years ago,
A catastrophic flood
Had swept away the chalk high ground
That linked England and France.

White cliffs of Dover were thence carved,
Exposing soft limestone,
Formed from planktonic green algae
That layered ocean floor.

Victorians thought to build a jail
So convicts work on harbour.
Eleven years it was there,
Yet prisoners sewed mailbags.

In wartime, cliffs were a frontline
Consisting large gun batteries.
They sheltered army troops onsite
In bomb resistant tunnels.

More than a half of UK coast
Is made up of tall cliffs.
Due to storm damage and rainfall
Some gradually retreat.

The winding solitary walks
Along the ancient ways
Reveal the wildlife habitats
Within the cliffs' vast swathes.

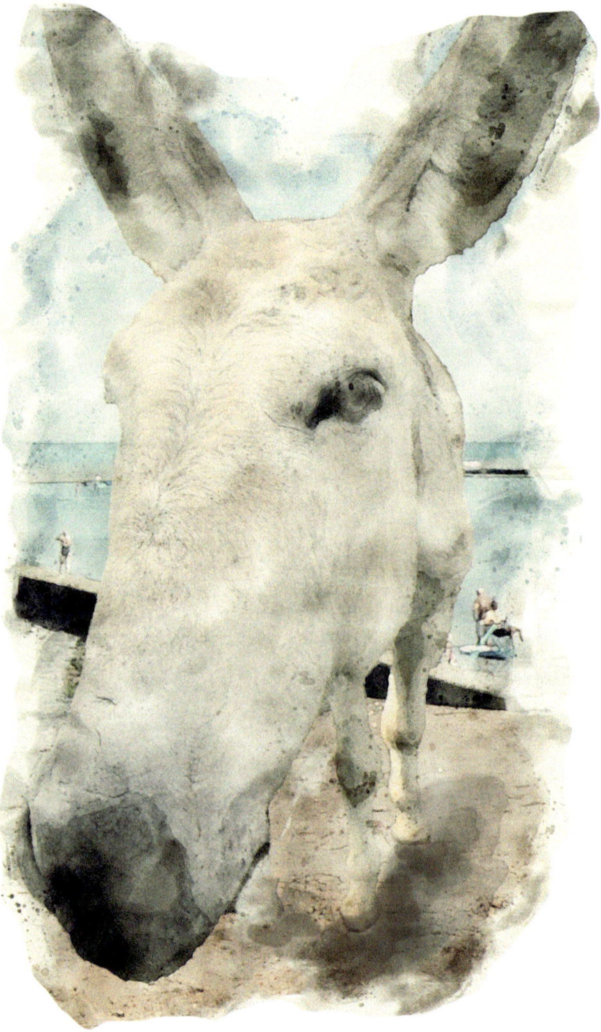

Inspired by donkey.

Donkey Ride

A popular holiday pastime—
To mount a donkey for a stroll,
Has been a presence at the seaside,
As the Victorians record.

The joy of ride on sandy shoreline
Drew children and the word had spread.
The rising number of the tourists
Added to seaside donkey trend.

Tradition is alive in summer;
Enhanced by welfare campaigns,
The ass is worked regular hours
With time to rest and water breaks.

After its labour years are over,
It heads to sanctuary in peace.
There, other retirees are grazing
And freely bray and snort, and squeal.

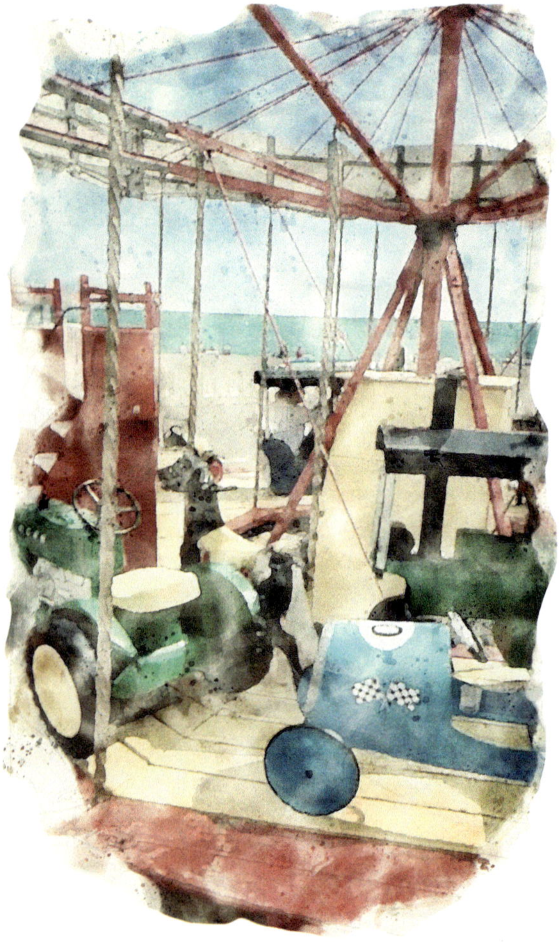

Inspired by rides in Ramsgate.

Fairground Rides

The bouncy castle, spin-and-swing boats,
The carousel and shooting range
Provide a day long entertainment
For seaside goers needing play.

The mix of cold polluted waters,
The jellyfish and seaweed clutch
Make paid for riveting alternative
A valid choice for fail-safe bash.

On weekend and holiday schedule,
The beaches buzz with children's laughs,
Only to go mute with bad weather,
Leaving a grim and empty site.

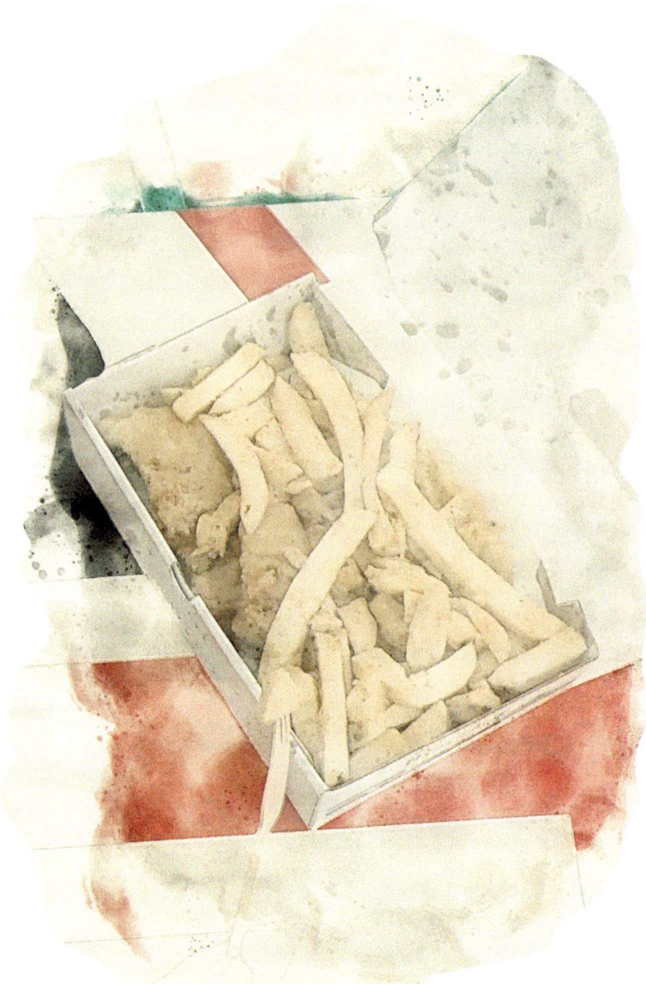

Inspired by fish and chips.

Fish and Chips

The culinary masterpiece
Of Great British cuisine—
The fish and chips withstood the time
As nation's favourite meal.

Believed to come from the East End
Whereby a Jewish immigrant
Sold battered fish, fried in flour coat,
To local cockney neighbourhood.

Meanwhile UK industrial north
Took fish with some potato chips,
Providing masses with comfort,
Described in 'Road to Wagan Pier'.

The rise of trawlers brought the fish
From all over Atlantic,
The railways allowed the dish
To be widely available.

Newspaper wrap helped keep price low
Until was ruled unsafe.
Now it is served in paper box
Or laid out on a plate.

Consumed with salt and vinegar,
And bowl of mushy peas,
The simple morsel finds its mouth
Across all-price-range chippies.

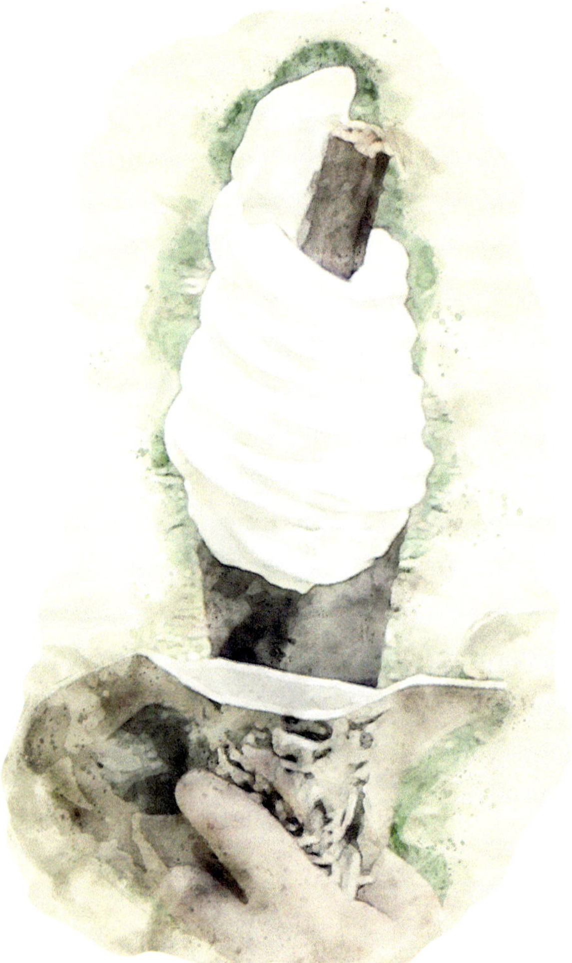

Inspired by Flake 99 ice cream.

Flake 99

Without a famous soft serve ice cream
No trip to seaside is complete.
With origins in coastal Scotland,
Its name is known to every kid.

After the WW1, an immigrant
With an Italian descent
Set up a parlour that was popular
And where he introduced the Flake.

99 Portobello High Street,
The shop's address where cone was sold,
Is said to explain '99' bit,
Albeit true meaning isn't known.

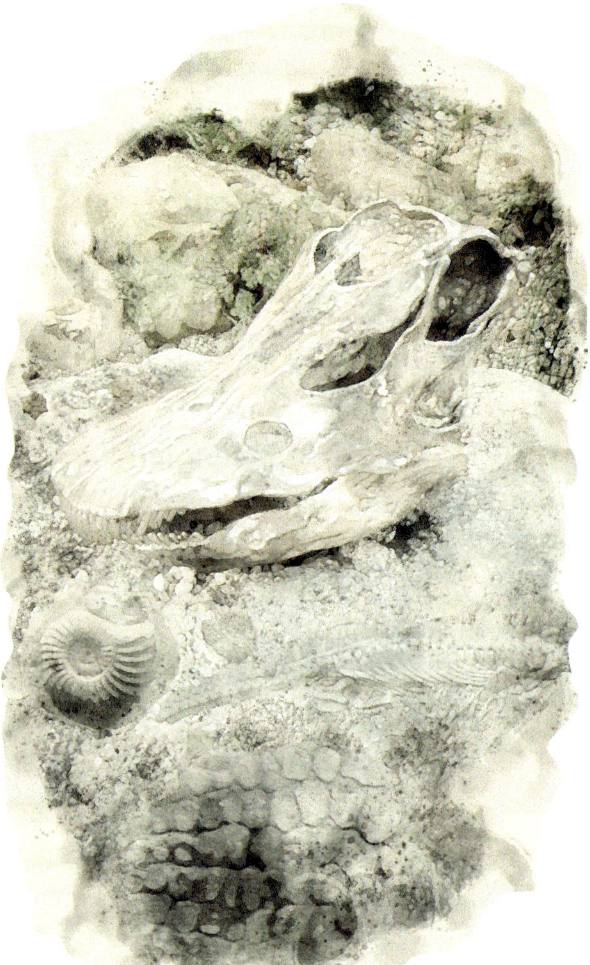

Inspired by various fossils in Natural History Museum.

Fossil Hunting

Remains of prehistoric presence
That survived into modern times,
Underwent partial preservation—
The harder parts got fossilised.

Millions of years of the process
Conserved fish skeletons, bird beaks,
Dinosaur bones, carbon impressions
Of long bygone flowers and leaves.

Paleonthologists recovered
Ichtyosaur vertebrae,
Sea monster skull, ammonites, nautili,
Among Jurassic coastal gems.

Beach combing, a seaside adventure,
With the correct terrestrial tools
May yield some creature's bone or denture,
Tree resin—amber, for the jewels.

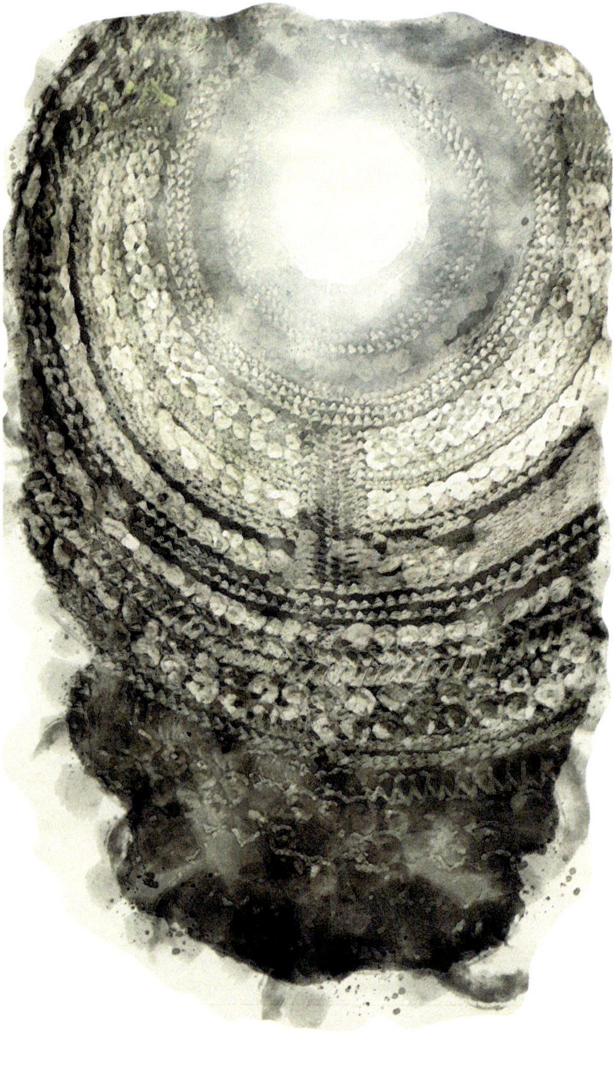

Inspired by Shell Grotto, Margate.
**Globe Theatre, London*

Oysters

The native oysters won the Romans
When they arrived and tried molluscs.
Consumed both as a treat and staple,
They were dominion's stock food.

The Medieval seaside dwellers
Snacked on the oysters by cartload.
Essential items for the poor,
Their shells were dug from under Globe*.

Boom in Victorian logistics
Allowed their movements far and wide.
British elite found them indulgent
So oyster farming had gold time.

With oystermen holding onshore pits,
The prices plunged for all involved.
The overfishing caused depletion,
Further disease drove pods extinct.

Technology had come to rescue,
The industry had a fresh start—
Beds were restocked; new cultivation
Has floating platforms and net bags.

Various types of aphrodisiac,
Farmed in Thames Estuary and Kent,
Are served across thousands of restaurants,
The seaside shacks and fishers' tents.

Inspired by Brighton Pier.

Pleasure Piers

At first, pieces of transport infrastructure
To help day-trippers reach the boat from shore,
The piers became the routes for promenading,
The places to fix health and score a glore.

The bandstands were setup for entertainment,
Amusement arcades, novelty and thrill,
Supported by the railway construction,
Brought visitors to new-built pleasure piers.

Eugenius Birch had fathered some fourteen piers—
Opulent forms with stresses and the girders,
That stood on bases fit for the lighthouses,
So strong, they called for later dynamiting.

Over a hundred specimens pierced waters,
Glowing at night, impressing their reflections,
Surviving deadly storms or, worse, succumbing,
Or burning down right to their foundations.

During wartime, to fend off the invaders,
The holes were blown, destroying solid structures.
Some fifty have survived and been refurbished,
Victorian magnificence they capture.

World's longest stretch of concrete, steel and iron,
Slits the Thames Estuary in buzzing coastal Southend.
The fairground rides attract the crowds to Brighton,
Southsea and Clacton, and Blackpool with Tower.

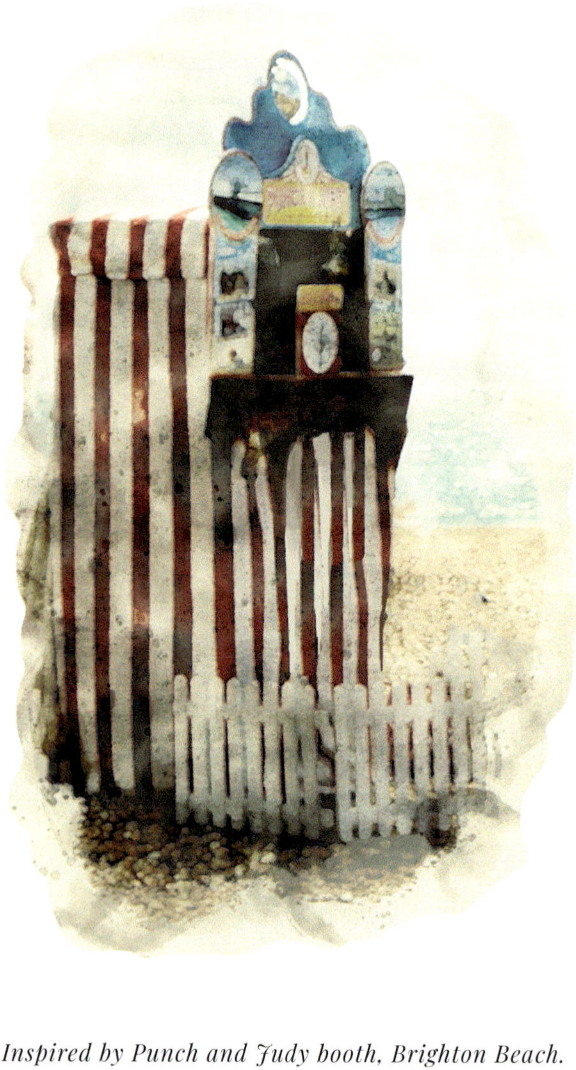

Inspired by Punch and Judy booth, Brighton Beach.
**Professor is the voice artist behind the show.*

Punch and Judy Puppet Show

A show that came from Gothic Italy,
Performed in Covent Garden live,
Was so impressive that the diarist,
Samuel Pepys, had seen it twice.

Commedia dell'Arte character,
Appealed to puppeteers and crowds.
Bright costumes, masks, colourful make up
Made 'Pulcinella', Mr Punch.

Unruly man carries a big club,
He beats offenders, dares his wife,
Troubles and tricks the law enforcement
And throws the baby when she cries.

The ancient practice of the 'swazzle',
Holding a whistle-like device
Inside the mouth of a professor*,
Creates a distinct squeaky sound.

Since Charles II, entertainment
Became phenomenally prized.
With the advent of modern railways,
It became staple of seaside.

Art form for ordinary people,
It reflects complex social cloth.
Despite attacks for being outdated,
In summertime it's going strong.

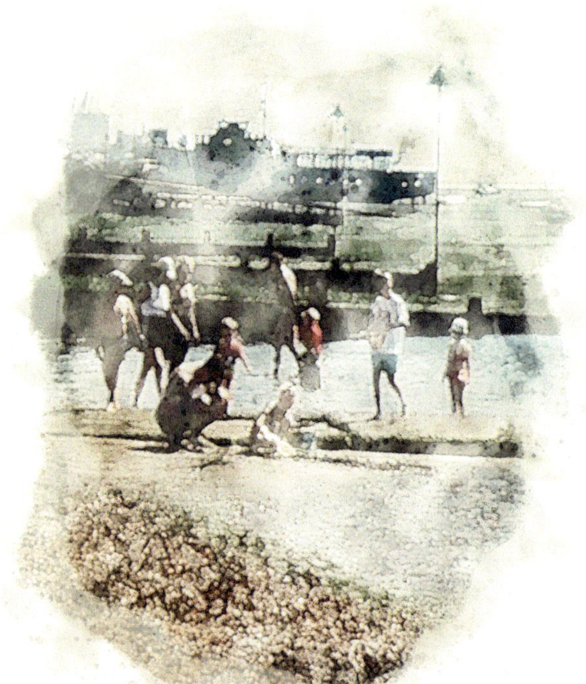

Inspired by beachside rock pooling.

Rock Pooling

On clear day, when tide is low,
The sheltered rocky shores,
Boulders and beaches slowly grow
With kids in rubber clogs.

Hunched over rock pools, they explore
The crabs and periwinkles,
Starfish, anemones, sea slugs,
The limpets and sea urchins.

Avoiding to intimidate
The creatures with their shadow,
They're keen to turn a rock or stone
To see what's hiding under.

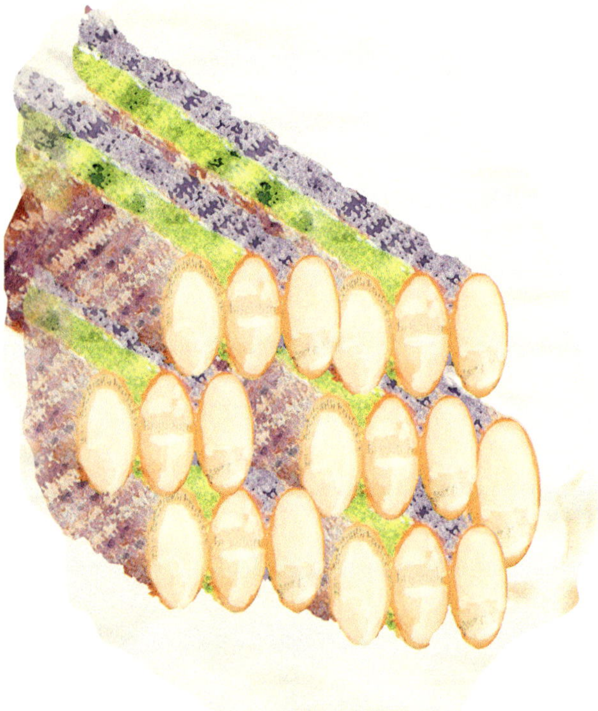

Inspired by various Sticks of Rock.

Stick of Rock

A hard boiled candy shaped like stick
And flavoured with a peppermint
Is an iconic British sweet
Produced by hand in mix of tints.

Common across seaside resorts,
The dainty includes reference
To the location where it's sold
By way of crafted lettering.

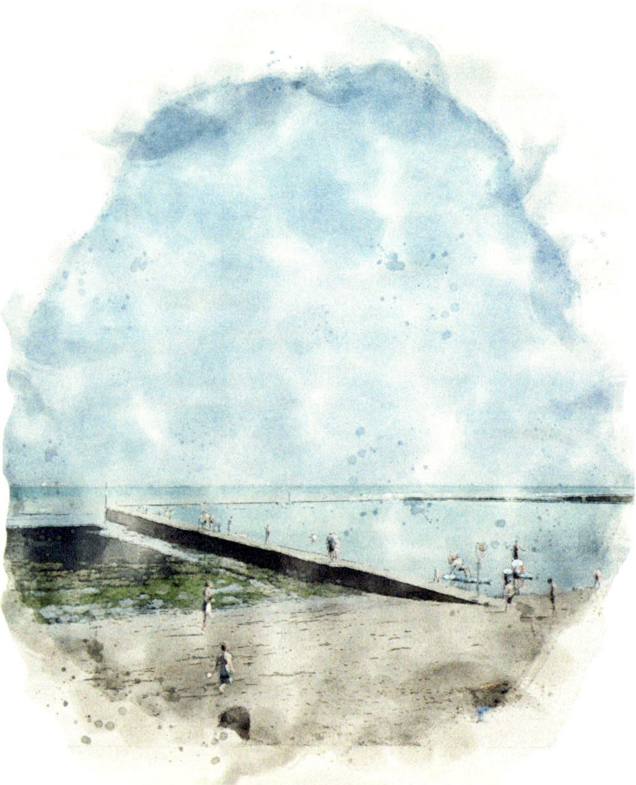

Inspired by tidal pool, Margate.

Tide

An inexperienced seagoer
May have been caught out by low tide
And spent the day messing on sand shores,
Not seeing water for some miles.

Britain's particular location
On Europe's Continental Shelf
Affords a mix of coastal landscapes
And fairly shallow water depths.

With Earth rotating on its axis,
The gravity pull of the Moon
Sets forth two giant waves at Land's End
That separate and meet, in turn.

One travels north to tip of Scotland,
Then it turns down towards East coast.
The other heads to English Channel;
At the Thames Estuary two merge.

The lunar day dictates the time gap
Between occurrence of the tide.
The complex cycle in Southhampton
Sees waters going double-high.

Forgetting to check tide timetable
Could force one to swiftly pack up,
Or end up dangerously stranded
Between safe exits to the banks.

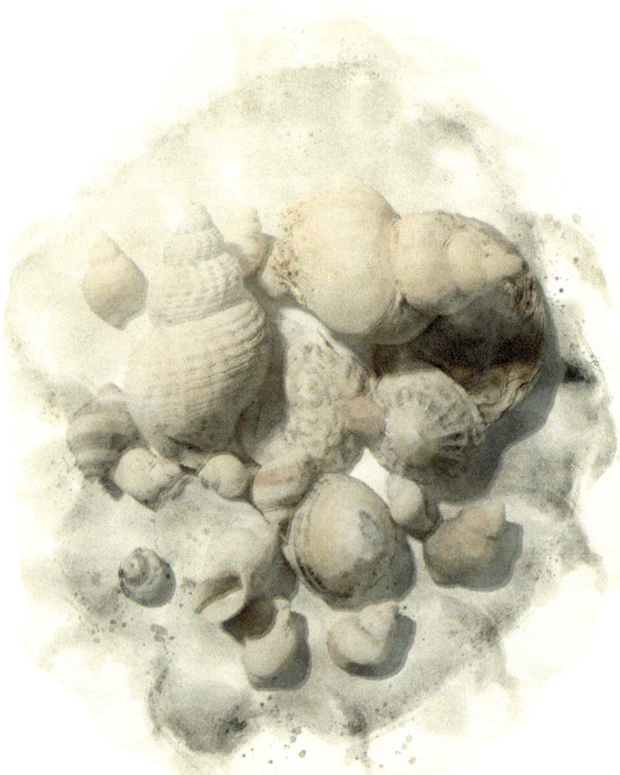

Inspired by shell treasures.

Treasures

A prominent English tongue-twister,
'She sells sea shells on a sea shore',
Ignores the local legal framework
For taking sea stuff from its lore.

Coastal Protection Act is clear—
Offenders are in for a fine
For pebble, shell or sand removal,
Regardless of the held amount.

It is, however, very legal
To collect rubbish like sea glass,
Contemporary life byproducts,
Especially the plastic bags.

Vast fortunes from the loot and pirates
Adorn the deep dark ocean floor,
Waiting their turn to be discovered
Washed up before the lucky soul.

The 'wreck'—the treasures washed on dry land
Belong to those who owned them first.
Keeping the finds equates to stealing,
The crime is—failure to report.

To curb the risk of apprehension,
The bucket content of the finds
Is ought to be replaced by driftwood
And other unprotected junk.

Enjoyed the book?

Please, dear reader, stay in touch,
Leave a review or two, share much.
And on that note—goodbye, adieu,
I will be glad to hear from you.

www.landejewels.com/contact

Scan for offers & previews!

Other books in the series

- Sights: what scenes may seem - ISBN: 9781739211547
- Bells: what tale bells tell - ISBN: 9781739211516
- Markets: why stall by stalls - ISBN: 9781739211523
- Birthday: what gifts day gives - ISBN: 9781739211530
- Wildlife: where wild freestyled - ISBN: 9781739211554
- Money: what the means mean - ISBN: 9781739211561
- Streets: what bred street cred - ISBN: 9781739211578
- Stations: where lines align - ISBN: 9781739211585
- Bridges: what ties allies - ISBN: 9781739211592
- Gravers : what bonds old bones - ISBN 9781917579018

Also available as Ebooks and some in Hardcovers

9781917579087

BV - #0067 - 270125 - C20 - 203/127/3 - PB - 9781917579087 - Gloss Lamination